Table of Contents

Welcome

Welcome to the English Department at Santa Rosa Junior College—and welcome to the department's customized handbook.

This opening section of the handbook provides essential information about the class you're currently taking, other English classes you may take later, resources on campus, and protocols and tips—from the College, from faculty, and from other students—to help you have the best academic experience possible. Take some time to browse the handbook's pages so that you're familiar with the kinds of information it offers.

We hope that your semester is wonderful, full of learning, new friendships, and discovery. We're glad you're here!

The English Department Office

Santa Rosa Campus: Emeritus 1648. 527-4351
Hours: M — Th 7:30 a.m. – 7:30 p.m.
        F 8:30 a.m. – 1:30 p.m.

When you need to turn in an assignment outside of class time and when your instructor is not holding office hours, take your work to the English Department Office. It is located in the middle section of the second floor of Emeritus. Be polite. Tell the staff that you need to leave an assignment for your instructor. (You'll need to know your instructor's name.) The staff will date-stamp the work, ask you if you need a receipt, and then put the work in the instructor's mailbox for you.

The office has a small staff, so it is closed if the staff is running an errand or in a meeting. If the office is closed when you arrive, drop your work through the mail slot of the door to the workroom (1651), directly across the hall from the English Department Office.

To leave work for your instructor on the Petaluma Campus, drop your papers in the Homework Box, which is attached to the wall outside of the Faculty Support Room, Room 631, in the Richard W. Call Classroom & Administration Building. The Homework Box is available any time the building is open. Campus staff retrieve work from the Homework Box roughly every hour and route it to instructors' personal mailboxes.

The English Department Writing Center

Petaluma Campus: 247A Kathleen Doyle Hall
Santa Rosa Campus: Emeritus 1629
For the current semester's hours, go to
http://www.santarosa.edu/english/wc_sr.html

The English Writing Center offers free, individual assistance for any writing assignment you have in any class. English faculty and Instructional Assistants are available for drop-in conferences to help you with any writing-related work, including brainstorming essay ideas, developing a thesis, using correct MLA (Modern Language Association) documentation format, and editing for grammatical and mechanical errors. The Writing Center also offers the use of computers for writing, research, and completing online learning modules. Limited free printing service is available for drafts of essays, college transfer applications, scholarship applications, and other college writing tasks.

The English Department Online Writing Lab (OWL)

http://www.srjcwritingcenter.com/lab.html

Developed by one of the English Department's faculty members, the Online Writing Lab (OWL) provides instruction on everything from tiny details about commas to the big picture of an entire essay. Categories of instruction include punctuation, grammatical sentences, clear sentences, paragraphs, essays, and research writing. Resources also include online video lessons featuring English Department faculty explaining many different writing issues, links to writing resources on the Web, and information about how to earn units while using the OWL.

The Benefits of Solid Reading & Writing Skills

When you study English, you develop skills that will serve you well in many professions. Studying English will strengthen your ability to read on many different levels. You will become more perceptive about language. Your thinking will become more discriminating. You will become adept at finding materials that you need — books, articles, Web sites, and audiovisual resources.

Regardless of the major you study and the work you choose to do, you will need first-rate language skills if you are to do well and advance in your profession. SRJC's Work Experience Department emphasizes the importance of language skills in the workforce (see SRJC-25). Reading, writing, speaking, and listening skills are the first item on its "21st Century Work Skills Objectives" form. That is, Sonoma County employers rank language skills as the most important asset that they're looking for in potential employees.

Also, there's evidence that stronger reading, writing, and thinking skills translate into larger salaries.

But there are many more benefits of studying English. You gain skills, but perhaps more importantly, you'll be exposed to beauty, ideas, and amazing stories. The study of English contains everything that people express and explore through the written word: love, history, observations about the natural world, beliefs about life's mysteries, family life, and justice.

ourses in the English pathway will introduce you to cademic discourse — the way language is used in higher ducation — to prepare you for success in college. While the pecific content of classes will vary, each course weaves ogether lessons on reading, writing, thinking, speaking, and nteracting that will increase in complexity as you move hrough the pathway. Courses are offered in a variety of ormats: traditional, online, and hybrid, and as part of the nany learning communities that the College offers. (For nore information, see the Student Programs section SRJC-5.) The *SRJC Catalog* and *Schedule of Classes* provide etailed information about courses, including when and where they are offered.

ENGLISH PATHWAY

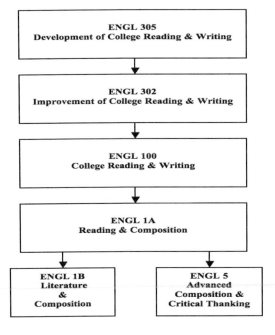

ENGL 305
Development of College Reading & Writing

ENGL 302
Improvement of College Reading & Writing

ENGL 100
College Reading & Writing

ENGL 1A
Reading & Composition

ENGL 1B
Literature
&
Composition

ENGL 5
Advanced
Composition &
Critical Thanking

Pathway Course Descriptions & Student Learning Outcomes

English 305: Development of College Reading and Writing

Catalog **Description**

Development of reading, writing, and information skills necessary for academic competency and career preparation at the college level.

Student Learning Outcomes

By the end of the semester, students will be able to demonstrate:

- Their knowledge of reading strategies and rhetorical patterns of organization
- Their ability to comprehend, interpret, analyze, and draw inferences from academic and career preparation texts
- Their ability to use the writing process to narrow a topic suitable for an essay of a prescribed length; formulate and develop a thesis with details, examples, and reasons; and express their ideas in clear and grammatical sentences and logical paragraphs
- Proficiency in reading comprehension

English 302: Improvement of College Reading and Writing

Catalog **Description**

Development of reading, writing, and information skills necessary for proficiency in academic and career-preparation college work.

Student Learning Outcomes

By the end of the semester, students will be able to demonstrate:

- An understanding of academic and career-preparation materials at a level required for but not ensuring success in English 100

- Proficiency in writing a variety of types of essays in response to readings and other materials required for but not ensuring success in English 100
- An ability to select and evaluate source materials and incorporate them correctly into writing assignments
- An ability to recognize and articulate the relationship between abstract concepts and particular facts

English 100: College Reading and Writing

Catalog Description

This course is designed to develop skills to the level required for success in ENGL 1A and other transfer-level courses.

Student Learning Outcomes

By the end of the semester, students will be able to:

- Analyze readings of various lengths and complexity in terms of rhetorical method of development, style, implications, irony, satire, assumptions, and biases
- Summarize and synthesize ideas from more than one college-level reading
- Apply the writing process to create logically developed and organized analytical essays with a clear point of view expressed in a thesis statement.
- Incorporate source materials and document them in MLA style

English 1A: Reading & Composition

Catalog Description

Critical reading and discussion of works in various literary forms. Composition predominantly of reasoned and reflective prose. Content and emphasis of particular sections specified in the English Department's course description bulletin "A Hundred Doors" issued every year.

Student Learning Outcomes

By the end of the semester, students will be able to:

- Write a comprehensive, well-developed, and coherent essay with a focused thesis and appropriate support
- Recognize and correct errors in grammar, punctuation, and spelling
- Identify and analyze argumentative, stylistic, and narrative techniques in nonfiction and fictional works
- Obtain, summarize, and synthesize research materials demonstrating the correct use of MLA citations

English 1B: Literature and Composition

Catalog **Description**

An introduction to literature that emphasizes critical reading, discussion, and analytic writing about works representative of fiction, poetry, drama, and literary criticism.

Student Learning Outcomes

By the end of the semester, students will be able to:

- Demonstrate reading skills that allow one to comprehend, analyze, and interpret works of fiction, literary nonfiction, poetry, and drama
- Apply one or more critical approaches to literature in well-developed, logically organized, and thesis-driven interpretive and analytical essays on widely recognized works of literature
- Identify and distinguish among the elements of a successful summary, response, analysis, and interpretation
- Demonstrate an appreciation of literary works whose aesthetic treatment of enduring human questions distinguishes them from those whose focus and purpose are primarily commercial

English 5: Advanced Composition and Critical Thinking

Catalog Description

A critical reasoning and advanced composition course designed to develop critical reading, thinking, and writing skills beyond the level achieved in English 1A. The course will focus on development of logical reasoning and analytical and argumentative writing skills.

Student Learning Outcomes

By the end of the semester, students will be able to:

- Describe principles of critical thinking
- Apply principles of critical thinking to texts, media, and everyday experience
- Write critical analysis and response papers

The Solkov Work of Literary Merit (WOLM)

http://www.santarosa.edu/english/current_wolm.html

Every semester, most instructors teaching English 1A set aside several weeks to read, discuss, and write about a work of literature that the department has selected. We call this the Work of Literary Merit, or WOLM for short. This work is usually a novel, but past WOLM picks have included collections of essays, stories, and poetry, as well as plays.

The department sponsors a lecture series on the selected work. These lectures are designed with you, the beginning college student, in mind. The lectures are interesting and accessible — not over the heads of college freshmen who may be learning about college-level literary analysis for the first time. Past WOLM events have also included an eighteenth-century country dance (for our work with Jane Austen's *Pride and Prejudice*), visits and lectures from the authors themselves (Maxine Hong Kingston, author of *The Woman Warrior*; and Greg Sarris, author of *Grand Avenue*), and essay contests (with prizes!).

The English Major

http://www.santarosa.edu (type "major" in the "Search" box, then choose "English" from the pull-down menu)

What do Dr. Seuss, astronaut Sally Ride, actor Christopher Reeve, novelist Stephen King, and San Diego Chargers coach Marty Schottenheimer all have in common? They were all English majors!

The English major fosters an appreciation of English and American literatures, as well as other literatures available in English translation. In addition to fulfilling requirements for an associate of arts degree, as an English major you can prepare for university transfer not only in English but in a variety of subjects requiring clear and creative expression, advanced reading and writing skills, and strong analytic ability. English majors also develop communication and interpretive skills highly valued in the workplace in a wide range of careers. Talk with a counselor for more information about majors.

Maps

Emeritus Hall, 2nd Floor, Santa Rosa Campus

1620	1624	1626	ENGLISH DEPARTMENT STAFF AND FACULTY OFFICES 1631-1668	DEPT. OF BEHAVIORAL SCIENCES OFFICES 1686-1690	1691	1692

1628 — 1614

1629 WRITING CENTER — 1610

1684 — 1678 — 1696

1564 NEWMAN AUDITORIUM — ELEVATOR — MEN — WOMEN

1607 | 1603 | 1601 — 1699 | 1697

SECOND FLOOR EMERITUS HALL

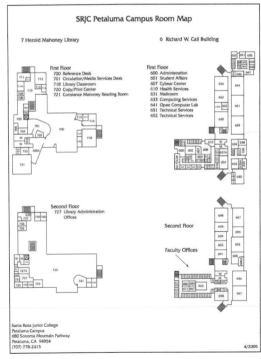

SRJC Petaluma Campus Room Map

7 Herold Mahoney Library

First Floor
700 Reference Desk
701 Circulation/Media Services Desk
718 Library Classroom
720 Copy/Print Center
721 Constance Mahoney Reading Room

Second Floor
727 Library Administration Offices

6 Richard W. Call Building

First Floor
600 Administration
601 Student Affairs
607 Cybear Center
610 Health Services
631 Mailroom
633 Computing Services
641 Open Computer Lab
651 Technical Services
652 Technical Services

Second Floor

Faculty Offices

Santa Rosa Junior College
Petaluma Campus
680 Sonoma Mountain Parkway
Petaluma, CA 94954
(707) 778-2415

4/2009

SRJC-13

Literature, Creative Writing, & the Literary Magazine

For a comprehensive list, course numbers, and course descriptions, see the *SRJC Catalog*.

Literature Courses

Genre courses focus on a particular literary form: Introductions to the Novel, Poetry, and the Short Story; Science Fiction; and Detective Fiction

Survey courses focus on the literature of a particular culture during a particular time in history: American Literature, European Literature, and British Literature.

Multicultural American literature courses focus on the literature of America's many ethnic subcultures: Ethnic Diversity, African American Arts and Literature, Asian American Literature, and Chicano/a Arts and Literature

Special focus courses are just that—they explore literature that has a particular emphasis: Literature and the Environment, Children's Literature, Mythic Themes, Women in Literature, Shakespeare, and Literature and Film

Creative Writing Courses

ENGL 4A: Beginning Creative Writing
ENGL 4B: Creative Writing Workshop
ENGL 4C: Advanced Creative Writing Workshop

The English Department's Literary Magazine (ENGL 80)

First Leaves: The Literary and Art Journal of Santa Rosa Junior College has been published since the spring of 1940. In 1974, English 80: Small Publications Workshop began to include not only the production of the journal but also instruction in various forms of printing and publications. Students who enroll in English 80 automatically become the staff of *First Leaves*.

English Department Scholarships & Awards

English Department Scholarships. The English Department is proud to honor its students each spring with a number of awards and scholarships, ranging from $300 to $950. For information about specific scholarships and deadlines, students should contact the SRJC Scholarship Office (Petaluma Campus: Kathleen Doyle Hall, 778-2461; Santa Rosa Campus: Plover Hall, 527-4740)

English Department Creative Writing Awards & Scholarships. In addition to the scholarships noted above, the English Department also sponsors scholarships based on the merit of students' creative writing submissions. For information about creative writing scholarships and deadlines, contact the English Department (Emeritus 1648, 527-4351).

Classroom Policies

English classrooms, like all classrooms, run smoothly when the teacher and students work collaboratively to establish and maintain a vibrant, engaging classroom environment. In order to sustain such an environment, it is necessary for the teacher and students to understand and follow the class policies and guidelines set forth in the course syllabus; these policies reflect the College's policies. The information below reflects SRJC's policies as outlined in the most recent *SRJC Catalog*, which can be located on the College's Web site at **http://www.santarosa.edu**. Click on the "Schedules and Catalog" link on the SRJC home page; you'll see an image for and a link to the current *SRJC Catalog*.

Student Responsibilities

Conduct yourself in a manner that encourages mutual respect, honorable behavior, and learning, thereby promoting student success and academic honesty.

Learn and understand the course requirements, grading procedures, expectations for acceptable conduct, definitions of plagiarism, and the ethical use of technology. Learn and understand SRJC policies on Academic Integrity and the Student Conduct Code, which are in the *SRJC Catalog*, section three, and part of Policy 8.2.8, Student Discipline. Be familiar with your syllabi so that you understand how these policies will be applied in your classes.

Learn and understand your rights to due process should you wish to contest an allegation or penalty made by an instructor or other representative of the College.

Attendance

You are expected to attend all sessions of the courses in which you are enrolled. The College does not require instructors to make a distinction between an excused or unexcused absence unless mandated by state or federal law. If you miss more than 10 percent of the total hours of class time or do not attend the first two class meetings, an instructor may drop you. For detailed information, see the *SRJC Catalog*, section three.

Classroom Behavior Expectations

Conduct yourself in a manner that encourages mutual respect, honorable behavior, and learning, thereby promoting student success and encouraging academic honesty. Refrain from any distracting behavior. Failure to do so will result in disciplinary action. Categories of misconduct that pertain to classroom behavior include dishonesty, such as cheating or plagiarism, and disruption of teaching or learning activities, including the use of vulgar or abusive language. For detailed information, see the *SRJC Catalog*, section three.

Personal Electronics

The use of cell phones, laptops, iPods, or other personal electronic devices can distract teachers and classmates, which negatively impacts the classroom environment. As noted above, disciplinary action can be taken for a variety of behaviors that disrupt teaching and learning activities, including the use of personal electronics. Check the course syllabus for your instructor's policies regarding personal electronics. When you are in the Writing Center, your cell phone must be turned off since this is a quiet work/study center.

Academic Integrity

Academic Integrity is the avoidance of all acts of academic dishonesty, which includes, according to section three of the *SRJC Catalog*, "any act of deception, benign or malicious in nature, in the completion of any academic exercise." Examples of academic dishonesty include but are not limited to plagiarism, cheating, falsifying records, or otherwise representing another's work as your own.

In classes that require writing and essays, it is especially important that you learn and understand exactly what plagiarism is so that you can avoid it. Plagiarism is presenting someone else's ideas or words as your own. To avoid plagiarism, you must cite all source material appropriately; in other words, give credit where it is due.

While some instances of plagiarism are unintentional, all instances of plagiarism are susceptible to disciplinary action. Check the course syllabus for your English instructor's plagiarism policy. If you are enrolled in other courses that require writing, be sure to ask those instructors about their plagiarism policies as well.

College Success Resources & Programs

Information and involvement: these two ingredients will enhance your SRJC experience, promoting both academic and personal success in college and beyond. SRJC is committed to your success and offers numerous support services to students and specialized programs to help you make decisions, make friends, and create a network of academic and social support. There is a service or program for every type of student. All of these services are described in detail on the SRJC Web site at **http://www.santarosa.edu** under the key link "For Students."

Please note that services and resources listed on the following pages will be housed in the new Lawrence A. Bertolini Student Services Center, which will open during the 2009-2010 academic year. The location of these services prior to their move to the Lawrence A. Bertolini Student Services Center is included in parentheses.

Student Services and Resources

Associated Students
http://www.santarosa.edu/for_students/as/

Petaluma Campus: Richard W. Call Classroom & Administration Building, Room 601
Santa Rosa Campus: Lawrence A. Bertolini Student Services Center (prior location: Pioneer Hall). 527-4424

SRJC Associated Students offers several opportunities to get involved in college life, which will enrich your academic experience. This office organizes campus activities and events and oversees student government and clubs. Join Associated Students to get involved and have fun.

arFacts

arFacts is a daily newsletter for students that provides dates about events, club meetings, job options, and much ore. It is a great resource if you're looking for a way to come involved in college activities.

reer Services

tp://www.santarosa.edu/for_students/student_resources/
reer-development-services/

nta Rosa Campus: Lawrence A. Bertolini Student Services
  Center (prior location: Bussman Hall, Room 1440).
  527-4941

e Career Center will help you explore and prepare for rious career fields and occupations through a variety of sources, such as career inventories, computerized career ting, and resume writing. It is never too early to explore e extensive resources the Career Center offers; the staff ill help you understand the relationship between the ajors you are considering and career opportunities. The nter also maintains a list of job postings in case you are eking a full- or part-time job, either on or off campus. On-mpus jobs give you an opportunity to develop useful job ills while working in a supportive environment. Off-mpus job listings are updated frequently and include a h variety of challenging and interesting opportunities.

Bear Center

tp://www.santarosa.edu/for_students/student_resources/
bear/

taluma Campus: Richard Call Hall, Room 607
nta Rosa Campus: Lawrence A. Bertolini Student Services
  Center (prior location: Pioneer Hall). 522-2638

e CyBear Center is a comprehensive copying and resource nter designed to help you with your academic projects. e center offers copying, scanning, laminating, and faxing services. You can also use the free workstations, which are supplied with staples, hole-punchers, paper cutters, correction fluid, pens and pencils, markers, paper clips, tape, and glue. Additionally, the CyBear Center issues photo IDs for use at College-sponsored events and in college libraries and computer labs.

Disability Resources Department (DRD)

http://online.santarosa.edu/presentation/page/?35762
Petaluma Campus: John M. Jacobs Hall, Room 101 778-2491
Santa Rosa Campus: Analy Village-C. 527-4278

SRJC has an excellent Disability Resources Department. If you have a disability and believe that you may need accommodations in any of your classes, contact DRD. Staff members advocate for students with disabilities, offering assessment, advising, classes, and tutoring.

English Department Writing Center

http://www.santarosa.edu/english/wc_sr.html
Petaluma Campus: 247A Kathleen Doyle Hall
Santa Rosa Campus: Emeritus 1629

For the current semester's hours, visit the Web site. The English Writing Center offers free, individual assistance for any writing assignment you have in any class. English faculty and Instructional Assistants are available for drop-in conferences to help you with any writing-related work, including brainstorming essay ideas, developing a thesis, using correct MLA documentation format, and editing for grammatical and mechanical errors. The Writing Center also offers the use of computers for writing, research, and completing online learning modules. Limited free printing service is available for drafts of essays, college transfer applications, scholarship applications, and other college writing tasks.

Extended Opportunity Programs and Services (EOPS)

http://www.santarosa.edu/app/paying-for-college/eops/
Santa Rosa Campus: Lawrence A. Bertolini Student Services
    Center (prior location: 1808 Albany Street, just off of
    Elliott Avenue). 527-4383

EOPS provides extensive assistance to full-time, low-income, educationally disadvantaged students so they can achieve their academic goals. This office provides academic, personal, and career counseling, priority registration, and book vouchers, as well as assistance with completing and submitting college forms.

Financial Aid Office

http://www.santarosa.edu/app/paying-for-college/
financial_aid_office/
Petaluma Campus: Kathleen Doyle Hall. (707) 778-2461
Santa Rosa Campus: Plover Hall. (707) 527-4471

SRJC offers several financial assistance programs, including numerous grants and loans, that may help you pay for your education. You must complete a Free Application for Federal Student Aid (FAFSA) to apply for any one of these programs.

Libraries at SRJC

http://www.santarosa.edu/library/
Petaluma Campus: Herold Mahoney Library. 778-3974
Santa Rosa Campus: Frank P. Doyle Library. 527-4391

We're extremely fortunate to have beautiful, new, state-of-the-art libraries on both campuses: Petaluma's Mahoney Library and Santa Rosa's Doyle Library. You will, of course, find a lot of books at both facilities. But what you may not know is that you'll also find media materials (DVDs, videos, audio recordings), art exhibits, and study rooms that can accommodate groups. The libraries have many computers for student use, as well as laptops that you can check out and use in the library. Both libraries have WiFi. We encourage you to take a tour of the library by checking out an iPod with an audio tour.

Besides visiting the physical libraries, you can also meet many of your research needs online through the library's extensive Web site. From the library's home page, you can access the book and media catalogs, online subscription databases, an extensive list of links to other Internet sites, and research resources for the current Work of Literary Merit (WOLM). The library's Web page also provides links to instructional Web sites and materials, library services, information about the library (for example, its hours and floor plans), and library news. It's a great resource! Spend some time becoming familiar with it.

Mathematics, Engineering, and Science Achievement (MESA)
http://www.santarosa.edu/mesa
Santa Rosa Campus: Lawrence A. Bertolini Student Services
    Center (prior location: Lark Temps). 521-7909

This SRJC program supports students who plan to obtain a bachelor's degree in a science, technology, engineering, or mathematical field. The MESA office offers academic excellence workshops, transfer assistance, a student study center, and professional development networking. For application information, contact the MESA office.

MyCubby Student Portal
http://www.santarosa.edu/index/shtml

MyCubby helps you stay informed in each of your classes. This user-friendly system enables you to receive class announcements, e-mail, and updates from your instructor. Login is required and easy to set up. To get started, click on the student portal link on SRJC's home page.

Scholarship Office

http://www.santarosa.edu/scholarship
Petaluma Campus: Kathleen Doyle Hall. 778-2461
Santa Rosa Campus: Plover Hall. 527-4740

SRJC's scholarship specialists are dedicated to helping you find the financial support necessary to help you reach your academic goals. The staff will assist you in researching and applying for one or more of the hundreds of scholarships offered at SRJC.

Student Health Services

http://www.santarosa.edu/for_students/student-services/ student-health-services
Petaluma Campus: Richard W. Call Classroom &
    Administration Building, Room 610. 778-3919
Santa Rosa Campus: Race Building, Room 4017. 527-4445

Student Health Services staff will help you understand the relationship between health and academic success. They can help you establish and maintain a healthy lifestyle conducive to achieving your educational goals. You don't have to wait until you have a cold to utilize their services; they offer many services, including health screenings, health advice, and psychological counseling.

Student Psychological Services

http://www.santarosa.edu/for_students/student-services/ services/services-available/#sps
Petaluma Campus: Richard W. Call Classroom &
    Administration Building, Room 610. 778-3919
Santa Rosa Campus: Race Building, Room 4017. 527-4445

This is one of the many specialized services offered through Student Health Services. The staff can assist you with any psychological stressors that are interfering with your academic and personal success. As a student at SRJC, you are eligible for short-term counseling, including individual, couples, family, and group therapy. If you are dealing with issues such as alcoholism, eating disorders, or stressful relationships, contact this office for assistance. It offers several screening and educational events related to these and many other issues.

Transfer Center

http://www.santarosa.edu/instruction/prepare_for_transfer/ resources/

Santa Rosa Campus: Lawrence A. Bertolini Student Services Center (prior location: Bussman Hall, Room 1434). 527-4874

If you are even considering the possibility of transferring to a four-year college or university, a visit to the Transfer Center is a must. Spend time with a transfer counselor to become familiar with the center's resources. This will help to make sure that your SRJC courses are truly preparing you for the four-year university or college you want to transfer to, as well as for the major you plan to study.

Tutorial Center

http://www.santarosa.edu/orientation/resources_academic.html#tutorial

Petaluma Campus: Richard W. Call Classroom & Administration Building, Room 690. 778-2409

Santa Rosa Campus: Frank P. Doyle Library, Room 4251. 521-6903

If you need assistance with any of your coursework, make the Tutoring Center a part of your weekly schedule. This center provides free tutoring and materials in numerous subjects including ASL, Astronomy, Biology, Business, Chemistry, Economics, English, ESL, History, Math, Philosophy, Physics, and other requested subjects. Drop-in tutoring is available for Math, Chemistry, and writing assignments.

Work Experience Department

http://www.santarosa.edu/instruction/jtwd/wei/
Petaluma Campus: John M. Jacobs Hall, Room 117. 778-3920
Santa Rosa Campus: Lawrence A. Bertolini Student Services
Center (prior location: 1440 Bussman Hall). 527-4329

The Work Experience Department offers a number of courses that help you develop the skills you will need in the 21st-century work world. Opportunities include internships, earning units while working, and volunteering. The faculty in the Work Experience Department focus on the skills that local, regional, and state employers are looking for in their employees. These skills include communication, customer service, time management, and teamwork, among others.

Student Programs

For current meeting times and dates for the following learning community and online courses, check the online *Schedule of Classes* by going to SRJC's home page at http://www.santarosa.edu/, opening the Quick Links menu, and selecting *Schedule of Classes*.

First-Year Experience (FYE) Courses

http://www.santarosa.edu/app/counseling/counseling-courses/

SRJC's Counseling Department provides two First Year Experience classes: Counseling 10 and Counseling 11. Both courses provide the academic and social support necessary to help you smoothly and successfully transition to a four-year college or university.

Learning Communities

http://www.santarosa.edu/app/getting-started/learning-communities/

SRJC's Learning Communities enhance your educational experience, helping you establish solid academic and social foundations that support your success. Instructors and students work together to build engaging learning-oriented environments to ensure that all participants make the most of their college experience. SRJC offers a First-Year Experience Learning Community, Puente Learning Communities, and several Interdisciplinary Learning Communities.

Online/Hybrid Classes

http://www.santarosa.edu/instruction/online-learning/index/shtml

SRJC offers a variety of online classes, providing an alternative to traditional classroom instruction and allowing you to learn from work or home. All online courses are taught by SRJC faculty, have the same rigor and quality as other SRJC classes, and employ methods of instruction that are customized to the online environment.

Puente Program

http://www.santarosa.edu/puente/about.shtml
Santa Rosa Campus: Lawrence A. Bertolini Student Services
  Center (prior location: Lark Temps). 524-1701

The Puente Program offers underserved students a yearlong English-Counseling Learning Community. The program's curriculum focuses on Latino literature and experiences. Puente students receive support, insight, and inspiration rom Puente mentors, individuals who have successfully navigated the road to university.

Study Abroad
http://www.santarosa.edu/sa

SRJC offers opportunities to study abroad in Costa Rica, London, Paris, and Florence. The purpose of the program, as stated on the Study Abroad Web site, is to "offer a variety of programs and services that will provide students, faculty, and the community at large with the knowledge, skills, and cultural experiences necessary to become well-prepared members of a global society."

Campus Maps

Santa Rosa Campus

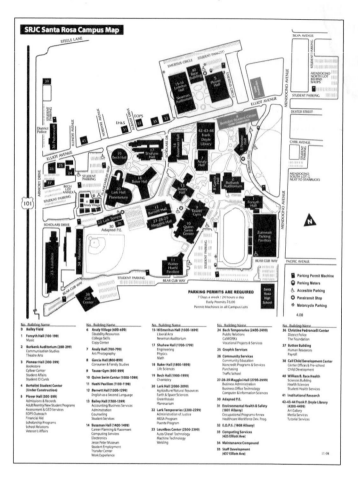

Petaluma Campus

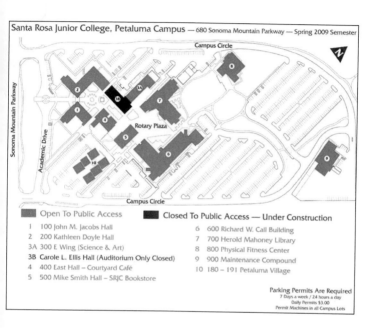

Santa Rosa Junior College, Petaluma Campus — 680 Sonoma Mountain Parkway — Spring 2009 Semester

Open To Public Access

1   100 John M. Jacobs Hall
2   200 Kathleen Doyle Hall
3A 300 E Wing (Science & Art)
3B Carole L. Ellis Hall (Auditorium Only Closed)
4   400 East Hall – Courtyard Café
5   500 Mike Smith Hall – SRJC Bookstore

Closed To Public Access — Under Construction

6   600 Richard W. Call Building
7   700 Herold Mahoney Library
8   800 Physical Fitness Center
9   900 Maintenance Compound
10 180 – 191 Petaluma Village

Parking Permits Are Required
7 Days a week / 24 hours a day
Daily Permits $3.00
Permit Machines in all Campus Lots

Useful Links

Art Gallery
http://www.santarosa.edu/for_students/student_resources/art-gallery/

CalWorks
http://www.santarosa.edu/app/paying-for-college/CalWORKs/

CyBear Center
http://www.santarosa.edu/for_students/student_resources/cybear/

SRJC Museum
http://www.santarosa.edu/museum/

Planetarium
http://www.santarosa.edu/planetarium/

SRJC Bookstore
http://www.santarosa.edu/bookstore/

Theatre Arts
http://www.santarosa.edu/theatrearts/

Veterans Affairs
http://www.santarosa.edu/app/paying-for-college/veterans-affairs/

Notes

PC Writing Center   Call 690

M 12:30 - 3:30
T 1:30 - 5:30
W 12:30 - 3:30
R 12:30 - 3:30

SR Emeritus 1629

M 9-3
T 9-5
W 9-5
R 9-3
F 10-1

PC Open Lab 641

M 9 - 7:50
T
W
R
F 9 - 1

Notes

SIXTH EDITION

Rules for Writers

Diana Hacker

Contributing Authors

Nancy Sommers
Tom Jehn
Jane Rosenzweig
Harvard University

Contributing ESL Specialist

Marcy Carbajal Van Horn
Santa Fe Community College

Bedford/St. Martin's
Boston ◆ New York

For Bedford/St. Martin's

Executive Editor: Michelle M. Clark
Development Editor: Mara Weible
Senior Production Editor: Anne Noonan
Production Supervisor: Jennifer Peterson
Senior Marketing Manager: John Swanson
Editorial Assistant: Alicia Young
Assistant Production Editor: Katherine Caruana
Copyeditor: Barbara G. Flanagan
Text Design: Claire Seng-Niemoeller
Cover Design: Donna Lee Dennison
Composition: Monotype Composition Company, Inc.
Printing and Binding: Quebecor World Eusey Press

President: Joan E. Feinberg
Editorial Director: Denise B. Wydra
Editor in Chief: Karen S. Henry
Director of Marketing: Karen Melton Soeltz
Director of Editing, Design, and Production: Marcia Cohen
Managing Editor: Elizabeth M. Schaaf

Library of Congress Control Number: 2009924669 (student edition)
2009924672 (tabbed student edition)

Manufactured in the United States of America.

3	2	1	0	9
e	d	c	b	a

For information, write: Bedford/St. Martin's, 75 Arlington Street, Boston, MA 02116
(617-399-4000)

ISBN-10: 0-312-59339-2   ISBN-13: 978-0-312-59339-1 (student edition)
ISBN-10: 0-312-59340-6   ISBN-13: 978-0-312-59340-7 (tabbed student edition)

Acknowledgments

Scott Adams, "Dilbert and the Way of the Weasel." Copyright © 2000 by United Features Syndicate. Reprinted with permission of United Media.
American Heritage Dictionary, definition for "regard" from *The American Heritage Dictionary of the English Language, Fourth Edition.* Copyright © 2006 by Houghton Mifflin Company. Reproduced with permission.
R. I. Berkowitz, T. A. Wadden, A. M. Tershakovec, and J. L. Cronquist, "Behavior Therapy and Sibutramine for the Treatment of Adolescent Obesity" from J*ournal of the American Medical Association* 289 (2003): 1807–1809. Copyright © 2003 by the American Medical Association. Reprinted with permission.
Eugene Boe, excerpt from "Pioneers to Eternity" from *The Immigrant Experience,* edited by Thomas C. Wheeler. Copyright © 1971 by Thomas C. Wheeler. Reprinted with the permission of Doubleday, a division of Random House, Inc.

Acknowledgments and copyrights are continued at the back of the book on page 592, which constitutes an extension of the copyright page. It is a violation of the law to reproduce these selections by any means whatsoever without the written permission of the copyright holder.

Preface for Instructors

Publisher's Note

> This book is grounded in my many years of teaching first- and second-year composition to a wide range of students: young and mature, mainstream and multiethnic, talented and underprepared. As I've drafted and revised *Rules for Writers,* my goal has never been to sell students on my own views about language and politics — or to endorse popular trends in the teaching of English. Instead, I've tried to look squarely at the problems students face and come up with practical solutions.
>
> —Diana Hacker, from the preface to
> *Rules for Writers,* Fifth Edition

First and foremost a teacher, Diana Hacker (1942–2004) was clear about why her handbooks have been so successful: They give students practical solutions to real writing problems. Her many innovations — both large and small — were always at the service of giving students the advice they need in a way they can understand. She was able to take everything she knew from her thirty-five years of teaching and put it to work on every page of her books. As a result, she was one of the most successful college textbook authors of all time, with her handbooks assigned at more than half of the two- and four-year colleges in the United States.

Of all of her handbooks, *Rules for Writers* was Diana Hacker's favorite; it was the one she assigned and taught from at Prince George's Community College. Her innovative quick-reference features were time-savers for her students, and her simplified, value-priced handbook option was a money-saver. In *Rules for Writers*, Diana and Bedford/St. Martin's had produced the best value in college publishing — a handbook that helped students answer all of their writing questions quickly and that was priced to fit any student's budget.

With a new team of coauthors, *Rules for Writers* still offers class-tested advice in a language students can understand and at a low price. In the Hacker tradition, the new contributing authors—Nancy Sommers, Tom Jehn, Jane Rosenzweig, and Marcy Carbajal Van Horn—have crafted solutions for the writing problems of today's college students. Together they give us a new edition that provides more help with academic writing and research and that works better for a wider range of multilingual students. And at Bedford/St. Martin's, we have worked hard to maintain the same high standards that have informed every Hacker handbook.

Joan Feinberg
President, Bedford/St. Martin's

Features of the Sixth Edition

What's new

NEW CHAPTER ON WRITING ABOUT TEXTS. Reading and responding to texts is a core skill for academic writing in any discipline. The new edition includes helpful guidelines for analyzing texts along with two new annotated samples—a summary and an analysis. New guidance for writing about visual texts helps students apply critical thinking skills when writing about advertisements, photographs, cartoons, and other visual media.

MORE HELP WITH WRITING ARGUMENTS. Revised coverage of counterargument teaches students how to strengthen their writing by anticipating and responding to objections. A new annotated sample paper demonstrates the effective use of counterargument.

NEW VISUALS TEACH CITATION AT A GLANCE. New full-color, annotated facsimiles of original sources show students where to look for publication information in a book, a periodical, a Web site, and a source accessed in a database. These visuals help students find the information they need to cite print and online materials accurately and responsibly.

ADVICE THAT HELPS STUDENTS MAINTAIN THEIR VOICE WHILE WRITING FROM SOURCES. Thoroughly revised coverage of integrating sources teaches students how to go beyond patchwork research writing. Section 56 shows students how to lead into — and get out of — sources while keeping the source material in context and maintaining their own line of argument.

MORE HELP FOR WORKING WITH SOURCES. New advice helps students determine what role each of their sources will play in their paper, a skill useful in composition and beyond. Students are encouraged to question whether a source will function as background material, expert testimony, counterargument, and so forth. Clear examples do the teaching.

NEW QUICK-ACCESS CHARTS. The sixth edition features new charts to help writers navigate common writing challenges: understanding a writing assignment, reading actively, analyzing visuals, determining scholarly sources, and avoiding Internet plagiarism.

MORE ESL HELP FOR GENERATION 1.5 STUDENTS. Thoroughly revised ESL coverage considers the experiences of college students who may be proficient English speakers but who continue to struggle with writing in English. The sixth edition offers stronger support — with handy charts and advice — for using verbs, articles, and prepositions correctly.

NOW WITH ADVICE ON ACADEMIC CONVENTIONS — FOR NATIVE AS WELL AS NONNATIVE SPEAKERS. New boxed tips teach *academic English* — or how to go about writing well at an American college. Throughout the book, these nuggets of advice — on topics such as plagiarism, writing arguments, and understanding writing assignments — help students meet college expectations.

NEW SAMPLE PAPERS. Two new research papers use current print and electronic sources and are annotated to show both good writing and proper formatting. The new MLA-style research essay examines Internet monitoring in the workplace, and the new APA-style paper is a review of the literature on treatments for childhood obesity. A new essay in section 46, "Writing about Texts," demonstrates effective analysis of an article.

NEW EXERCISE ITEMS. Revisions of two hundred exercise items reflect a diversity of experience and offer practice through high-interest topics. These new items, along with the existing ones, provide students abundant opportunities for practice on every topic in the handbook.

What's the same

We have kept the features that have made *Rules for Writers* work so well for so many students and instructors. These features, detailed here, will be familiar to users of the previous edition.

A BRIEF MENU AND A USER-FRIENDLY INDEX.   Designed for student use, a brief menu inside the front cover displays the book's ten parts and lists only the numbered sections. The traditional, more detailed handbook menu, which is useful for instructors but too daunting for many students, appears inside the back cover.

The handbook's index (which Diana Hacker wrote herself and which was carefully updated for this edition) helps students find what they are looking for even if they don't know grammar terminology. When facing a choice between *I* and *me,* for example, students may not know to look up "Case" or even "Pronoun, case of." They are more likely to look up "*I* " or "*me,*" so the index includes entries for "*I* vs. *me*" and "*me* vs. *I.*" Similar user-friendly entries appear throughout the index.

QUICK-REFERENCE CHARTS.   Many of the handbook's charts help students review for common problems in their own writing, such as fragments and subject-verb agreement. Other charts summarize important material: a checklist for global revision, strategies for avoiding sexist language, guidelines for evaluating Web sites, and so on.

EXTENSIVE EXERCISES, SOME WITH ANSWERS.   At least one exercise set accompanies nearly every grammar section of the book. Most sets begin with five lettered sentences with answers in the back of the book so students can test their understanding independently. The sets then continue with numbered sentences whose answers appear only in the Instructor's Edition. Students who need more practice can go to the book's companion Web site (see pp. xvii–xviii for details).

DISCIPLINE-SPECIFIC RHETORICAL ADVICE FOR MLA AND APA STYLES. Advice on drafting a thesis, avoiding plagiarism, and integrating sources is illustrated for both documentation styles — MLA and APA — in color-coded sections. Examples are tied to topics appropriate to the disciplines that typically use each style: English and other humanities for MLA and social sciences and health professions for APA.

What's on the companion Web site
<http://dianahacker.com/rules>

RESOURCES FOR WRITERS AND TUTORS. New writing center resources on the companion Web site offer help for both tutors and writers: checklists for responding to a wide array of assignments, tips for preparing for a visit to the writing center, hints for making the best use of advice from tutors, and helpsheets for common writing problems—the same kinds of handouts students see in the writing center—all available in printable format.

GRAMMAR EXERCISES. For online practice, students can access more than one thousand exercise items—on every grammar topic in the handbook—with feedback written by Diana Hacker. Most of the exercises are scorable. Exercises that call for editing are labeled "edit and compare"; students are asked to edit sentences and compare their versions with possible revisions.

RESEARCH AND WRITING EXERCISES. Scorable electronic exercises on matters such as avoiding plagiarism, integrating sources, using MLA and APA documentation, and identifying citation elements give students ample practice with these critical topics. Scorable exercises on thesis statements, peer review, point of view, transitions, and other writing topics support students throughout the composing process.

EXTRA HELP FOR ESL WRITERS. For native and nonnative speakers alike, this area of the site offers advice and strategies for understanding college expectations and for writing well on college assignments. It includes many helpful charts, exercises and activities, advice for working with sources, and an annotated student essay.

LANGUAGE DEBATES. These twenty-two brief essays encourage students to explore controversial issues of grammar and usage (such as split infinitives and *who* versus *whom*), think about the rationales for a rule, and then make their own rhetorical decisions.

MODEL PAPERS. Model papers for MLA, APA, *Chicago,* and CSE styles illustrate both the design and the content of researched writing. Annotations highlight key points about each paper's style, content, and documentation.

RESEARCH AND DOCUMENTATION ONLINE. This online resource helps students conduct research and document their sources. Reference librarian Barbara Fister has updated her advice on finding sources and has provided new links to resources in a variety of disciplines. Guidelines for documenting print and online sources in MLA, APA, *Chicago,* and CSE styles are also up-to-date.

ACCESS TO PREMIUM CONTENT. With the purchase of a print version of the handbook, students can access premium content including an e-book version of *Rules for Writers* as well as a series of tutorials.

Ancillaries for students

Both print and electronic ancillaries are available for students.

PRINT RESOURCES

Developmental Exercises to Accompany RULES FOR WRITERS

Answers to Exercises in RULES FOR WRITERS

Working with Sources: Exercises to Accompany RULES FOR WRITERS

Research and Documentation in the Electronic Age, Fourth Edition

Language Debates, Second Edition

Extra Help for ESL Writers

Writing about Literature

Writing in the Disciplines: Advice and Models

Designing Documents and Understanding Visuals

ONLINE RESOURCES

Rules for Writers companion Web site (see pp. xvii–xviii)

Comment with *Rules for Writers*

Ancillaries for instructors

Classroom and professional resources for instructors are available in print form. Other resources appear on the instructor portion of the book's companion Web site.

PROFESSIONAL RESOURCES FOR INSTRUCTORS

Teaching Composition: Background Readings

The Bedford Guide for Writing Tutors, Fourth Edition

The Bedford Bibliography for Teachers of Writing, Sixth Edition

WEB RESOURCES FOR INSTRUCTORS

Rules for Writers instructor site < http://dianahacker.com/rules/instructor >

- Exercise Masters, print-format versions of all the exercises in the book
- Quiz Masters, print-format quizzes on key topics in the book
- Electronic Diagnostic Tests, a test bank for instructors' use
- Transparency Masters, useful charts, examples, and visuals from the book
- *Preparing for the CLAST*
- *Preparing for the THEA*

In addition, all of the resources within *Re:Writing* < http://bedfordstmartins.com/rewriting > are available to users of *Rules for Writers.* Resources include tutorials, exercises, diagnostics, technology help, and model documents — all written by our most widely adopted authors.

Acknowledgments

We called on a number of individuals to help us develop the sixth edition with Diana Hacker's goals as a foundation.

Contributors

The following contributing authors brought expertise, enthusiasm, and classroom experience to the revision. They wrote new content and rethought existing content to make certain that *Rules for Writers* reaches a broader range of students and meets their various needs. Nancy Sommers, Tom Jehn, and Jane Rosenzweig helped revise the coverage of the writing process, writing about texts, and research. Marcy Carbajal Van Horn revised the ESL coverage.

Nancy Sommers, Sosland Director of Expository Writing at Harvard University, has also taught composition at Rutgers

University and at Monmouth College and has directed the writing program at the University of Oklahoma. Diana was a longtime admirer of Nancy Sommers's work because it focused on student writing. A two-time Braddock Award winner, Nancy is well known for her research and publications on student writing. Her articles "Revision Strategies of Student and Experienced Writers" and "Responding to Student Writing" are two of the most widely read in the field. Her recent work involves a longitudinal study of undergraduate writing.

Tom Jehn teaches composition and directs the writing across the disciplines program at Harvard University. A recipient of numerous teaching awards both at Harvard and at the University of Virginia, he also leads professional development seminars on writing instruction for public high school teachers through the Calderwood Writing Fellows Project.

Jane Rosenzweig, a published author of fiction and nonfiction, teaches composition and directs the writing center at Harvard University. She has also taught writing at Yale University and the University of Iowa.

Marcy Carbajal Van Horn, assistant professor of English and ESL at Santa Fe Community College (FL), teaches composition to native and nonnative speakers of English and teaches the advanced ESL writing course. She has also taught university-level academic writing and critical thinking at Instituto Technológico y de Estudios Superiores in Mexico. Marcy creates practical and accessible content for a broad range of students — starting with her own — as Diana always did.

Reviewers

For their many helpful suggestions, we would like to thank a perceptive group of reviewers.

Eileen Abel, Bluegrass Community and Technical College

James Beasley, DePaul University

Lisa Beckelhimer, University of Cincinnati

Allegra Blake, Central Michigan University

Christina Bowman, California State University, Long Beach

Addison Bross, Lehigh University

Elaine Brousseau, Providence College

Cynthia L. Butos, Trinity College

Anita L. Cook, Bridgewater College

Susan Jean Cooper, College of the Canyons

Diana Federman, Holyoke Community College

Deborah Fleming, Ashland University

Douglas B. Hoehn, Community College of Philadelphia

Noha Kabaji, Golden West College

Elana Kent-Stacy, College of the Canyons

Mary T. Lane, Anne Arundel Community College

Benjamin Lareau, Casper College

Maurice L'Heureux, Northern Virginia Community College

Deborah B. Luyster, University of North Florida

David Marlow, University of South Carolina Upstate

Mark R. Matthews, Anne Arundel Community College

D. Erik Nielson, Northern Virginia Community College

Denee Pescarmona, College of the Canyons

Anne M. Rector, Emory University

Angela D. Schlein, University of Florida

Leta McGaffey Sharp, University of Arizona

Ann L. Smith, Modesto Junior College

Catherine Sutton, Ithaca College

Carol Ann Theuer, Wake Technical Community College

Amy Ulmer, Pasadena City College

Donald Wildman, Wake Technical Community College

Cynthia Schoolar Williams, Tufts University

Student contributors

We are indebted to the students whose essays appear in this edition—Jamal Hammond, Luisa Mirano, Anna Orlov, Emilia Sanchez, and Matt Watson—not only for permission to use their work but also for allowing us to adapt it for pedagogical purposes.

Our thanks also go to the students who granted permission to use their paragraphs: Celeste Barrus, Rosa Broderick, Diana Crawford, Jim Drew, Connie Hailey, Craig Lee Hetherington, William G. Hill, Linda Lavelle, Kathleen Lewis, Laurie McDonough, Chris Mileski, Leon Nage, Julie Reardon, Kevin Smith, Margaret Smith, Margaret Stack, John Clyde Thatcher, and David Warren.

Bedford/St. Martin's

Rules for Writers had always been a team effort between Diana Hacker and her editors at Bedford/St. Martin's. The Hacker team is still in place. Joan Feinberg, president, was the editor on the first editions of every Hacker handbook, including *Rules for Writers*, and has been a part of every book since. Special thanks go to Chuck Christensen for understanding what makes a great handbook author and for knowing he had found one in Diana Hacker. At the heart of the Hacker team is Diana's longtime editor, executive editor Michelle Clark, the most skilled, creative editor we could wish for. Development editor Mara Weible expanded the new media offerings, making them as easy to use as the book itself. Claire Seng-Niemoeller has designed every Hacker handbook since the first and has again retained the clean, uncluttered look of the book while making more use of color. Having copyedited every Hacker handbook, Barbara Flanagan has helped to develop the clarity and consistency that is a Hacker hallmark. Senior production editor Anne Noonan kept the team on track with her persistence, sharp eye, and concern for every detail. Assistant production editor Katie Caruana provided detailed assistance throughout the page proof review. Editor in chief Karen Henry and managing editor Elizabeth Schaaf have worked on these books from the beginning and remain committed to maintaining the high level of quality of Hacker handbooks. Editorial assistant Alicia Young managed various projects and made sure that we heard from many users. The team remains committed to maintaining the high level of quality of Hacker handbooks.

How to Use This Book and Its Web Site

Though it is small enough to hold in your hand, *Rules for Writers* will answer most of the questions you are likely to ask as you plan, draft, and revise a piece of writing: How do I choose and narrow a topic? What can I do if I get stuck? How do I know when to begin a new paragraph? Should I write *each was* or *each were*? When does a comma belong before *and*? What is the difference between *accept* and *except*? How do I cite a source from the Web?

The book's companion Web site extends the book beyond its covers. See pages xvii–xviii for details.

How to find information with an instructor's help

When you are revising an essay that has been marked by your instructor, tracking down information is simple. If your instructor marks problems with a number such as *16* or a number and letter such as *12e,* you can turn directly to the appropriate section of the handbook. Just flip through the orange tabs at the top of the pages until you find the number in question. The number *16,* for example, leads you to the rule "Tighten wordy sentences," and *12e* takes you to the subrule "Repair dangling modifiers." If your instructor uses an abbreviation such as *w* or *dm* instead of a number, consult the list of abbreviations and revision symbols on the next to the last page of the book. There you will find the name of the problem (*wordy; dangling modifier*) and the number of the section to consult.

How to find information on your own

With a little practice, you will be able to find information in this book without an instructor's help — usually by consulting the brief menu inside the front cover. At times, you may consult the detailed menu inside the back cover, the index, the Glossary of Usage, the list of revision symbols, or one of the directories to documentation models. The tutorials on pages xix–xxii give you opportunities to practice finding information in different ways.

THE BRIEF MENU.   The brief menu inside the front cover displays the book's contents as briefly and simply as possible.

Let's say that you are having problems writing parallel sentences. Your first step is to scan the menu for the appropriate numbered topic — in this case "9 Parallelism." Then you can use the orange tabs at the top of the pages to find section 9. The information in the tabs — the section number and the symbol for parallelism — will tell you that you are in the section you need.

THE DETAILED MENU.   The detailed menu appears inside the back cover. When the numbered section you're looking for is broken up into quite a few lettered subsections, try consulting this menu. For instance, if you have a question about the proper use of commas after introductory elements, this menu will lead you quickly to section 32b.

THE INDEX.   If you aren't sure which topic to choose from one of the menus, consult the index at the back of the book. For example, you may not realize that the issue of whether to use *have* or *has* is a matter of subject-verb agreement (section 21). In that case, simply look up "*has* vs. *have*" in the index and you will be directed to specific pages in two sections covering the topic of subject-verb agreement.

THE GLOSSARY OF USAGE.   When in doubt about the correct use of a particular word (such as *affect* and *effect, among* and *between,* or *hopefully*), consult the Glossary of Usage at the back of the book. This glossary explains the difference between commonly confused words; it also lists words that are inappropriate in formal written English.

DIRECTORIES TO DOCUMENTATION MODELS. When you are documenting a research paper with MLA or APA style, you can find documentation models by consulting the appropriate directories. For MLA in-text citation and works cited directories, see the pages marked with a vertical band of orange; for APA in-text citation and reference list directories, see the pages marked with a vertical band of gray.

How to use this book and its Web site for self-study

In a composition class, most of your time will be spent writing. So it is unlikely that you will study all of the chapters in this book in detail. Instead you should focus on the problems that tend to crop up in your own writing. Your instructor (or a tutor in your college's writing center) can help you design a program of self-study.

Rules for Writers has been designed so that you can learn from it on your own. By providing answers to some exercise sentences, it allows you to test your understanding of the material. Most exercise sets begin with five sentences lettered a–e and conclude with five numbered sentences. Answers to the lettered sentences appear in an appendix at the end of the book.

The following list describes the features on the book's companion Web site < dianahacker.com/rules >. Each feature — whether an electronic exercise or a Language Debate or a writing center helpsheet — has been developed for you to use on your own whenever you need it.

ON THE WEB dianahacker.com/rules

> **Writing exercises**
  Interactive exercises on topics such as choosing a thesis statement and conducting a peer review

> **Grammar exercises**
  Interactive exercises on grammar, style, and punctuation

> **Research exercises**
  Interactive exercises on topics such as integrating quotations and documenting sources in MLA and APA styles

> **Model papers**
  Annotated sample papers in MLA, APA, *Chicago*, and CSE styles

ON THE WEB (continued)

> **ESL help**
Resources and strategies to help nonnative speakers improve their college writing skills

> **Language Debates**
Mini-essays exploring controversial issues of grammar and usage, such as split infinitives

> **Research and Documentation Online**
Advice on finding sources in a variety of disciplines and up-to-date guidelines for documenting print and online sources in MLA, APA, *Chicago*, and CSE styles

> **Tutorials**
Interactive resources that teach essential skills such as integrating sources in MLA style and writing paraphrases and summaries

> **Resources for writers and tutors**
Revision checklists and helpsheets for common writing problems

> **Additional resources**
Print-format versions of the exercises in the book and links to additional online resources for every part of the book

Tutorials

The following tutorials will give you practice using the book's menus, index, Glossary of Usage, and MLA directory. Answers to the tutorials begin on page 578.

TUTORIAL 1
Using the directories

Each of the following "rules" violates the principle it expresses. Using the brief menu inside the front cover or the detailed menu inside the back cover, find the section in *Rules for Writers* that explains the principle. Then fix the problem. Examples:

> *Tutors in*
> ~~In~~ the writing center,/ ~~they~~ say that vague pronoun reference is
>
> unacceptable. *23*
>
> *come*
> Be alert for irregular verbs that have ~~came~~ to you in the
>
> wrong form. *27a*

1. A verb have to agree with its subject.
2. Each pronoun should agree with their antecedent.
3. About sentence fragments. You should avoid them.
4. Its important to use apostrophe's correctly.
5. Check for *-ed* verb endings that have been drop.
6. Discriminate careful between adjectives and adverbs.
7. If your sentence begins with a long introductory word group use a comma to separate the word group from the rest of the sentence.
8. Don't write a run-on sentence, you must connect independent clauses with a comma and a coordinating conjunction or with a semicolon.
9. A writer must be careful not to shift your point of view.
10. When dangling, watch your modifiers.

TUTORIAL 2
Using the index

Assume that you have written the following sentences and want to know the answers to the questions in brackets. Use the index at the back of the book to locate the information you need, and edit the sentences if necessary.

1. Each of the candidates have decided to participate in tonight's debate. [Should the verb be *has* or *have* to agree with *Each*?]
2. We had intended to go surfing but spent most of our vacation lying on the beach. [Should I use *lying* or *laying*?]
3. We only looked at two houses before buying the house of our dreams. [Is *only* in the right place?]
4. In Saudi Arabia it is considered ill mannered for you to accept a gift. [Is it okay to use *you* to mean "anyone in general"?]
5. In Canada, Joanne picked up several bottles of maple syrup for her sister and me. [Should I write *for her sister and I*?]

TUTORIAL 3
Using the menus or the index

Imagine that you are in the following situations. Using either the menus or the index, find the information you need.

1. You are Ray Farley, a community college student who has been out of high school for ten years. You recall learning to put a comma between all items in a series except the last two. But you have noticed that most writers use a comma between all items. You're curious about the current rule. Which section of *Rules for Writers* will you consult?
2. You are Maria Sanchez, a peer tutor in your university's writing center. Mike Lee, a nonnative speaker of English, has come to you for help. He is working on a rough draft that contains a number of problems with articles (*a, an,* and *the*). You know how to use articles, but you aren't able to explain the complicated rules on their correct use. Which section of *Rules for Writers* will you and Mike Lee consult?
3. You are John Pell, engaged to marry Jane Dalton. In a note to Jane's parents, you have written, "Thank you for giving Jane and myself such a generous contribution toward our honeymoon." You wonder if you should write "Jane and I" or "Jane and me." What does *Rules for Writers* say?
4. You are Selena Young, an intern supervisor at a housing agency. Two of your interns, Jake Gilliam and Susan Green, have writing problems involving -*s* endings on verbs. Jake tends to drop -*s* endings; Susan tends to add them where they don't belong. You suspect that both problems stem from nonstandard dialects spoken at home.

Susan and Jake are in danger of losing their jobs because your boss thinks that anyone who writes "the tenant refuse" or "the landlords agrees" is beyond hope. You disagree. Susan and Jake have asked for your help. Where in *Rules for Writers* can they find the rules they need?

5. You are Joe Thompson, a first-year college student. Your friend Samantha, who has completed two years of college, seems to enjoy correcting your English. Just yesterday she corrected your sentence "I felt badly about her death" to "I felt bad about her death." You're sure you've heard many educated people, including professors, say "I felt badly." Upon consulting *Rules for Writers,* what do you discover?

TUTORIAL 4
Using the Glossary of Usage

Consult the Glossary of Usage to see if the italicized words are used correctly. Then edit any sentences containing incorrect usage. If a sentence is correct, write "correct" after it. Example:

The pediatrician gave my daughter a̶ *an* injection for her allergy.

1. Changing attitudes *toward* alcohol have *effected* the beer industry.
2. It is *mankind's* nature to think wisely and act foolishly.
3. This afternoon I plan to *lie* out in the sun and work on my tan.
4. Our goal this year is to *grow* our profits by 9 percent.
5. Most sleds are pulled by no *less* than two dogs and no more than ten.

TUTORIAL 5
Using the directory to MLA works cited models

Assume that you have written a short research essay on the origins of hip-hop music. You have cited the following sources in your essay, using MLA documentation, and you are ready to type your list of works cited. Turn to page 437 and use the MLA directory to locate the appropriate models. Then write a correct entry for each source and arrange the entries in a properly formatted list of works cited.

A book by Jeff Chang titled *Can't Stop, Won't Stop: A History of the Hip-Hop Generation.* The book was published in New York by St. Martin's Press in 2005.

An online article by Kay Randall called "Studying a Hip-Hop Nation." The article appeared on the University of Texas at Austin Web site, which you accessed on October 13, 2008. The last update was October 9, 2008.

A journal article by H. Samy Alim titled "360 Degreez of Black Art Comin at You: Sista Sonia Sanchez and the Dimensions of a Black Arts Continuum." The article appears in the journal *BMa: The Sonia Sanchez Literary Review*. The article appears on pages 15–33. The volume number is 6, the issue number is 1, and the year is 2000.

A sound recording entitled "Rapper's Delight" performed by the Sugarhill Gang on the CD *The Sugarhill Gang*. The CD was released in 2008 by DBK Works.

A magazine article accessed through the database *Expanded Academic ASAP*. The article, "The Roots Redefine Hip-Hop's Past," was written by Kimberly Davis and published in *Ebony* magazine in June 2003. The article appears on pages 162–64. You found this article on October 13, 2008.

Contents

Document Design 59

Clarity 79

Grammar — 147

ESL Challenges   223

Academic Writing   345

Basics